FACES of FISHING

FACES of FISHING

PEOPLE, FOOD AND THE SEA AT THE BEGINNING OF THE TWENTY-FIRST CENTURY

BRADFORD MATSEN

FOREWORD BY JULIE PACKARD

MONTEREY BAY AQUARIUM PRESS

For Ray Troll, JAV

*The mission of the Monterey Bay Aquarium
is to inspire conservation of the oceans.*

Published in the United States by the Monterey Bay Aquarium
Foundation, 886 Cannery Row, Monterey, CA 93940-1085.
www.mbayaq.org

Library of Congress Cataloging in Publication Data:
    Matsen, Bradford
        Faces of fishing: people, food, and the sea at the beginning of
        the twenty-first century / Bradford Matsen.
        p.   cm.
    Includes index.
    ISBN 1-878244-20-5 (pbk. : alk. paper)
    1. Fishery resources. 2. Fishery conservation. 3. Food supply.
    4. Fisheries—Pictorial works. I. Title.
SH327.5.M38 1997   97-36387
33.95'6—dc21   CIP

PHOTO CREDITS:
Cover: Robb Kendrick/Aurora; Aw, Michael: 8, 79, 85 (bottom left);
Azel, Jose: 23, 55, 116, 117; Balthis, Frank S.: 5, 18, 20-21, 38-39, 46-47, 75
(top right), 81 (top left & bottom left); Braasch, Gary: 120, back cover;
Browne, Rick: 49, 72, 73, 74, 75 (left), 80, 81 (bottom right), 82;
Chamberlain, Marc: 62 (bottom); Curtsinger, Bill: 7, 16, 43 (left), 65 (top
right), 115; Essick, Peter/Aurora: 50; Hall, Howard: 41, 85 (right);
Heimann, Anne: 43 (right), 100, 101; Essick, Peter/Aurora: 111; FAO: 64,
65 (top left), 65 (bottom); Fitzgerald, Roger: 10-11, 51; Fobes, Natalie B.: 9,
19, 24, 26, 27, 29, 83, 84, 85 (top left), 92-93, 94-95, 96-97, 103, 104, 105 (top),
108, 109; Foott, Jeff: 52; Kazmers, Marilyn/Innerspace Visions: 22;
Kendrick, Robb/Aurora: 3, 4, 6, 12, 14, 15, 17, 30-31, 32, 33, 36, 37, 40, 48, 56-
57, 58, 59, 60, 61, 62 (top), 62-63, 66-67, 68, 69, 75 (bottom right), 76, 77, 81
(top right), 88, 89, 98, 99, 102, 105 (bottom), 106-107, 112-113, 114;
Mangurian, David/Inter-American Development Bank: 53; Matsen,
Bradford: 13, 25, 28, 34, 35, 45; McCloskey, William: 78; Muller, Thomas:
91, 110; News, Darien: 44; Pinneo, Joanna B./Aurora: 90; Perrine,
Doug/Innerspace Visions: 1; Sartore, Joel/National Geographic
Society: 42; Stanfield, James L./National Geographic Society: 86-87

Design: Elizabeth Watson
Managing Editor: Nora L. Deans
Project Editor: Lisa M. Tooker

Printed in Hong Kong through Global Interprint

ACKNOWLEDGMENTS

I wish to thank Martha Campbell, Don Doering, Dayton Alverson, Mercedes Lee, Steve Webster and Jenny Sayre Ramberg for their efforts in reviewing this book. Special thanks to Thea Sagen who did the original photo research for the "Fishing For Solutions: What's the Catch?" exhibit where we first saw these incredible images and the potential for producing this book. I am also indebted to Jane Lubchenco, Gary Neilsen and his crew, Max McCarty and Noel Pallas, my colleagues at *National Fisherman* magazine, and, not least, Nora Deans, Lisa Tooker, Betty Watson and everyone else at Monterey Bay Aquarium Press who worked hard to bring this book into the world.

—Brad Matsen

▲ *Cabugan Island, Phillipines.*

In 1984, the Monterey Bay Aquarium opened on Cannery Row in Monterey, California. Located on the site of what was once the largest sardine cannery, we had the great fortune to interpret one of the most pristine and diverse marine habitat areas in the north Pacific—Monterey Bay. A decade later, twenty-two million people have experienced our exhibits, and the bay itself is now protected as the nation's largest national marine sanctuary. But the legacy of overfishing remains in the broken-down cannery buildings, one by one being overtaken by a new economic base—tourism—in place of a once-bustling fishing industry.

We've learned little from history lessons like these. Despite years of management efforts, the vast majority of our world fisheries are being fished at or beyond sustainable levels. An additional large segment carry the ominous description "Status Unknown." Our numbers—and our drive for ocean food and commerce—are growing at an unprecedented pace. We must act quickly to insure a sustainable future for ocean life, and for ourselves.

This volume is based on images drawn together for an exhibition we created at the aquarium designed to raise public awareness of these very issues. Called "Fishing for Solutions: What's the Catch?," the exhibition seeks to illustrate the problems, and potential remedies, facing our world fisheries.

It is often said that "a picture's worth a thousand words," and we found the images collected for the exhibit to be so compelling, we wanted to share them with a broader audience. They illustrate the human side of conservation, and the tremendous challenges we face in balancing human needs with healthy ecosystems. They remind us of our vital connection with the sea. And most importantly, they reflect the power of the human spirit, our ultimate key to meeting the challenges ahead.

CONTENTS

▲ *On the Pacific coast, near Magadan, Russia.*

◄◄ *A fish market in India, one of the many countries where ocean protein is crucial for survival as well as commerce.*

▲ *The salmon runs in Bristol Bay, Alaska are healthy because of tight management and the absence of a large human population.*

Faces of Fishing

*"One of the great dreams of man must be to find
some place between the extremes of civilization and nature
where it is possible to live without regret."*

—Barry Lopez

 Gary Neilsen, on the grounds off Kodiak.

In February, 1987, a year before we officially figured out that the ocean was not an endless source of food, Gary Neilsen took me fishing. In the darkness of an Arctic morning, I rode with him in his pickup along the wrinkled hillside over Kodiak to his trawler, *Royal Baron*, and a week on the Gulf of Alaska. The weather for a change was decent; cold but calm and dry. His girlfriend, Shirley, was there on the seat beside him, cowboy-close with her arm draped across his shoulders. And over the noise of the heater fan, I heard them talk about the weather and intimacies in the secret codes of couples of long standing. Gary and Shirley were in their early thirties then; he, the adopted son of a fisherman, and she a bookkeeper at one of the dozen fish plants chugging away in the richest fishing town on earth. They couldn't find a way to make love last and are no longer together, but that morning they were wound tightly to each other and the sea in the embrace of optimism that a lot of fishing people know about. Good fishing is like nothing you can describe to a landsman, a blinding miracle of skill and luck that makes everything else in your life joyful. "It was one of those rare moments," Gary would tell me later, "when the

Good fishing is like nothing you

can describe to a landsman, a blinding

miracle of skill and luck that makes

everything else in your life joyful.

▲ *Beach fishing on Bristol Bay, Alaska.*

I told stories about crabbers on

the Bering Sea who made more

money in a month of brutal fishing

than most people make in a year . . .

little guy was poised to make some real money. And I got to come home every few days."

The cab of the truck smelled like dog, motor oil and cigarettes, elemental aromas in a fisherman's rig, and the bed behind us was a heap of line, pink buoy balls, engine parts, groceries and our duffels. I was going fishing to write about Gary, his boat and his life for a magazine which, like him, depended for its survival entirely on the continued abundance of the sea.

I had been a fisherman, too, a salmon troller in Southeast Alaska, and loved the life so much I would have done it forever for nothing. But I loved my daughter more, and the eight-month seasons were too long for my version of fatherhood. Writing about fishing, though, turned out to be the next best thing to making a living at it.

For the next seventeen years, I would sail with trawlers, crabbers, shrimpers, gillnetters, trollers and longliners all over the Pacific, beat it back to my domestic confines, and write about them. I told stories about crabbers on the Bering Sea who made more money in a month of brutal fishing than most people make in a year, salmon fishermen who savored the bucolic life of free-roaming independent hunters and Athabaskan trap fishermen on the Yukon River. I sat through fisheries management meetings that were as arcane and glacial as amateur operas, and watched the Americans, Norwegians, Germans, Russians, Japanese, Koreans, Danes and British bring the power and hubris of the industrialized world to every fishing ground on earth. The time was freighted with tension, as that rush to develop efficient, industrial fishing fleets collided with the emerging sensibilities of environmentalism. Since we had seen the *Apollo* moonship photograph of the whole earth, the finite blue speck on which we all live, extracting resources without restraint was obviously folly.

Gary Neilsen was, among other things, successful at staying alive and turning a profit on one of the nastiest oceans on earth, and already had survived the collapses of shrimp and king crab in his home waters, along with the cyclic variations of salmon. He took up trawling when his father turned the *Royal Baron* over to him with an admonition: "You'd better catch fish." And he did. According to family legend, a proud-hearted Gary cruised back into town on one of his first trips with his hold full of Pacific cod, the deck swamped with fish and a full net in tow like a plump, giant sausage.

Gary was an early rider on the industrial wave that swept over the North Pacific grounds, triggering $2 billion of global investment in the world's biggest fleet of trawlers, factory trawlers, factory longliners, motherships and shore plants. On a global scale, though, just as that crest of money rolled through booming fishing ports from Seattle to Dutch Harbor, the sea cried, "Enough." The message was loud, clear and shocking, a raw bolt from the planet that struck the heart of a human population that, until then, had only whispered the truth in the most abstract terms: We are outrunning our food supply. We have exploited every niche for agriculture and grazing and now we know that the sea won't feed all of us forever. The ocean, it turns out, probably won't sustainably produce much more than ninety million metric tons of food for human consumption and animal feed a year no matter how much horsepower we throw at it. If we overfish, we will get less. (Responsible aquaculture might produce another fifteen to twenty million tons.) The American stampede to the still-healthy cod, pollock and flatfish stocks off Alaska, therefore, would be the last of its kind.

Until then, the idea of an inexhaustible ocean, like any other admirable and serviceable fiction about natural resources, contained some truth and a lot of comfort. Just about everybody figured that the sea could keep up with the hunger of a human population that had doubled in forty years

▲ *Red salmon, Bristol Bay, Alaska.*

The ocean ... probably won't sustainably produce much more than ninety million metric tons of food for human consumption and animal feed a year ...

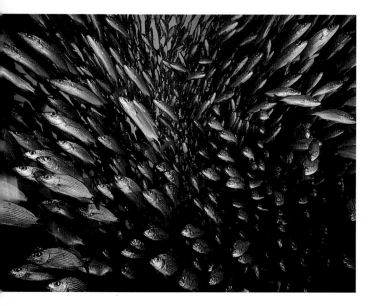

▲ *A school of snapper off the Pacific coast of Costa Rica.*

When I was a kid in the 1950s,

My *Weekly Reader* in school blithely declared

that billions of tons of seafood were there

for the taking, with no end in sight.

and showed no sign of slowing down. We are no more able to live comfortably with the specter of millions of starving people than we would be with a firm date for a killer earthquake or asteroid. But what do we tell the children who have to live with an uncertain legacy that already includes hunger and might mean global famine if they just do the math? When I was a kid in the 1950s, My *Weekly Reader* in school blithely declared that billions of tons of seafood were there for the taking, with no end in sight. By the mid-seventies, though, slightly better science revised that estimate to about five hundred million tons. (Scientists inside the industry, of course, were doing the estimating and they needed development, too.) Still, no sweat at dinnertime, and it was full-speed ahead on developing wide-open fisheries with no need for restraint. In 1989, though, with the news of the ninety million metric ton upper limit to the ocean's sustainable food production, we finally knew the truth, and only then did the fiction look worn and foolish.

To that point, fishing and all our interactions with our food were founded upon the assumption of endless supply, a paradigm that created economics based on constant development. To Gary Neilsen and fishermen around the world, you just moved on to the next best fishery when the one you were in dried up. This had been true for all of human history in Alaskan waters, the archipelagos of the China Sea, on the African coast and everywhere else people depended for survival upon protein from the marine food web. The strategy, for centuries, was eat, move, go broke or starve. The difference now, of course, is that there is nowhere to run to.

That week in February aboard the *Royal Baron* with Gary Neilsen, I watched him catch forty tons of Pacific cod and carefully bleed every one in backbreaking days on deck with his two crewmen. They stowed the fish below in chilled sea water to deliver perfect food to the plant in town.

Then, for almost a week, we waited out a wicked gale at anchor in the shelter of Ugak Bay, a tectonic stretch mark that fractures the southern coast of Kodiak where the island confronts the Aleutian Trench. We played cribbage, ate all day when we weren't beachcombing, told lies and stories about earlier fishing trips and argued fish politics. A decade earlier, when I was fishing, nobody I knew ever set foot inside a meeting room. Topics for wheelhouse debate did not include limiting access to the grounds, closing fisheries, dividing up quotas in Solomonic decisions that leave no one satisfied or plans for quitting fishing or maybe getting into ecotourism. Aboard *Royal Baron*, all were bitter daily fare.

Gary's journeyman deckhand was a fortyish Aleut who carried cultural sarcasm like a newspaper rolled up under his arm, and he didn't hesitate to use it to make a point. He was descended from one of the thousands of family bands that were nourished in harmony by the abundance of the North Pacific until just a few generations ago when the Russians, and then the Americans, threw their long, civilized shadows over the place. As we argued fisheries allocations, quotas and limits, he swatted us over and over with the folly and hypocrisy of an industrial culture that isolates people from their food supply but won't let him shoot seals to eat. He'd say things like, "Trucks stop running, L.A. starves." Or, "You hammered the shrimp, you hammered the crab, you'll hammer the codfish. Wait and see. You got no way to know when to stop."

And off we'd go into defense and speculation about codfish, eating king crab and shrimp or keeping the Kodiak fleet safe from the coming horde of big factory ships that could suck up a whole season's fish in a couple of months. Alone there on Ugak Bay in 1987, swinging on our anchor, we couldn't really know that fishermen fighting about dividing up the catch was roughly akin to moving the deck chairs around on the

▲ *Three generations of Oregon coast fishermen.*

"You hammered the shrimp,

you hammered the crab, you'll hammer

the codfish. Wait and see. You got no

way to know when to stop."

▲ *Salmon seining, Johnstone Strait, British Columbia.*

Titanic. It can keep you busy for awhile, but you're still headed for the bottom. A year later, though, everybody in the fishing world, from the booming Alaskan grounds to the reefs dying off the Philippines to the offshore tuna fleets would begin to know the astonishing truth.

It came in a United Nations report, one of those often-numbing collections of statistics and bad prose that could replace tranquilizers in a pinch. This one, though, from the Food and Agriculture Organization, brought every economist, politician, food theorist and, of course, fisherman around the world to attention. Here's the short version: From 1950 to 1989, the global catch of edible protein from the oceans, lakes and rivers increased steadily from about twenty million metric tons to about ninety million metric tons. Then, despite increased fishing capacity and a flood of capital investment, the catch stopped growing, as if it had hit an ecological wall. And here's the kicker. In the mid-1990s, the business of fishing still ran at a net loss against capital investment. To catch $70 billion worth of fish each year, the world's fishermen, their governments and bankers are pumping $124 billion into building ships and boats, buying fuel and gear and paying crews and other operating costs. As a global economic community, we are losing $50 billion a year and allowing the pressure to produce a return on that out-of-whack investment to threaten the health and sustainability of a big part of our food supply. Seventy percent of the world's fish stocks are either overfished or right at the limit of their capacity to produce sustainable yields. To sustain fisheries, we have to leave enough fish in the water to allow them to replace themselves, especially when they are at low points in their biological cycles for reasons other than human predation.

▲ *Payday on Bristol Bay.*

In 1989, . . . despite increased fishing

capacity and a flood of capital investment,

the catch stopped growing, as if it

had hit an ecological wall.

◂◂ *Mexican sardine fishermen along the coast of Baja California, Mexico.*

▴ *A fisherman and his wife with their catch of stingray off the coast of Baja California, Mexico.*

Food, the Sea and Feedback Loops

Local fishermen in Monterey, California.

How did this happen? Just pointing the finger at fishermen, we are starting to realize, is akin to blaming the messenger if we don't like the message. The real problem is that, since the post-war rush to the fishing grounds, people who eat fish were leading lives that were vastly different from those who caught them. From that remote anchorage on Ugak Bay, for instance, we steamed into Kodiak and delivered a boatload of Pacific cod to a processing plant. There, the fish were washed, sorted and frozen for shipment to Portugal, ten thousand miles away, where they would be sold to people who had no idea who caught the codfish or where it hatched, grew and died. This means that the consumer of that cod was not confronted with the responsibility for preventing overfishing, waste, overcapitalization or the destruction of the habitat the food needs to live. If the Portuguese broker can't get codfish from Alaska, then cod from Newfoundland tastes just fine, especially since nobody thought we'd ever run out of new places to fish.

While runaway fisheries development suffers from the absence of community responsibility on a scale as grand as the shiny new fleets, the nonindustrial, or artisanal, fisheries can be destructive, too. Most of them now are overfished and many are further threatened by modern distant-water fleets fishing the same waters. Nearly half the seafood in the world comes from those small-scale coastal fisheries, but is consumed by people who eat it within a few miles of the beach or dock where it came ashore. The people who depend on that food are much more closely connected to its source. If they overfish, they know about it quickly and either figure

Nearly half the seafood in the

world . . . is consumed by people who

eat it within a few miles of the beach or

dock where it came ashore.

▲ *Along a stream in Japan, Ainu fishermen perform a traditional salmon ceremony for a television crew, though they haven't been allowed to catch salmon there for over forty years.*

Since the last retreat of the ice from the

northern latitudes 14,000 years ago, salmon

and people have been locked in an embrace

that encircles the Pacific Rim . . .

out how to fish sustainably or miss a lot of meals. The feedback loop connecting irresponsible fishing with deprivation or death is local, a matter of concern for the entire community and not just the people doing the actual fishing.

It's pretty amazing to watch what happens when people rally around a fish to form what amounts to a communal band. On another magazine assignment that turned into a teachable moment, I followed a salmon from the deck of a fishing boat in Alaska, where it died, to a restaurant table a thousand miles away in Seattle where a half-dozen celebrants ate it and told salmon stories. Salmon are perfect food, but even more poignantly, they inspire the story of the deep bonds we share with them, with the coasts, rivers and streams they inhabit, with the sea that creates life, with the true community we share. Since the last retreat of the ice from the northern latitudes 14,000 years ago, salmon and people have been locked in an embrace that encircles the Pacific Rim from what is now Southern California, up the coast past Alaska and the Aleutian chain, and south all the way to the Korean peninsula. In every culture, people remind themselves of the source of this precious food in ceremonies and remembrances that are remarkably similar. Most involve catching a salmon, preparing it in the traditional way, eating together and returning the remains of the fish to the sea.

This particular fish was a Copper River king, a twenty-pound package of life born in the upper reaches of the watershed that drains into eastern Prince William Sound, a magnificent hen-salmon, lush with the urgent promise of the next generation. In the sweet home gravel of a deep eddy, her ancestors passed life into her in that familiar symphony of egg and sperm shared by all animals. And then luck and instinct took over. As a two-year-old juvenile, she had found the ocean with millions of her cousins, migrating down the free-flowing river facing upstream, as salmon do. Statistically, she would be an anomaly when she reached tidewater, the charmed and hardy survivor of a winter in a frozen river, swarms of trout and Dolly Varden that needed her food right then for their own lives, and the gulls, eagles, egrets, herons and other birds that guard the passage through the great delta. For three years she had been at large, hunting in the Pacific gyre until her genetic song called her to return to the river, guiding her journey with a blend of geomagnetic navigation and a sense of smell more acute than that of a dog.

The fishermen were a couple of middle-aged men who had eased through the counterculture days; one in a farmhouse in Walla Walla, the other as a traveling bartender. Each had come to Alaska to fish with a friend, made more money than he thought possible in a few weeks, bought his own boat and never left the Sound. "I've had as much fun as anybody," one of them said, unselfconsciously making a foray into his own history. "I graduated from college; I cooked on a wood stove; I drove a pickup with a big engine; I went fishing. I'll tell you, it just doesn't get any better than this."

Cordova, their home port, would a few years later become part of the American lexicon of the evening news after the *Exxon Valdez* made fools of us all on a reef just a few miles up the Sound. That day we were fishing the flats, though, the place had been a mining-town-gone-sour, resurrected by the more even-tempered economics of fishing. Almost everyone came from someplace else, almost everyone fished for salmon, crab and halibut and most thought they were lucky to have found the place, which is why they took the tanker accident so personally. I was on the Sound during that terrible time, too, riding with fishermen who rushed first to try to contain the spill, then to deal for years with the nauseating aftermath. On

▲ *Max McCarty and Noel Pallas, Copper River salmon fishermen.*

"I graduated from college; I cooked

on a wood stove; I drove a pickup with a

big engine; I went fishing. I'll tell you,

it just doesn't get any better than this."

▲ *The aftermath of the* Exxon Valdez *disaster, Green Island, Alaska.*

A diner . . . could savor a meal of [a]

salmon caught 72 hours earlier on the Copper

River Flats . . . but rarely knew more about

this salmon than the name of the river.

one particular dawn as we stood in the wheelhouse watching the sunrise over the grounded ship, a fisherman said something like this to me: "I don't blame Joe Hazelwood or Exxon; I blame everybody who is at the wheel of a car, commuting this morning in L.A. or Chicago or wherever. Gas doesn't cost a buck twenty a gallon, it costs this."

The salmon that flood the 300,000-acre delta of the Copper River, its rivulets and tributaries are the *Beaujolais nouveau* of the annual spawning migration that gives the coasts of the Pacific Rim their abundant character. They are the first, and, many say, the best of the new runs. Their rich color and high oil content quite simply define "salmon" for discriminating chefs, diners and backyard cooks. In the 1980s, Copper River salmon harmonized with the care of fishermen and packers, ingenious marketing and the miracle of the jet plane. A diner in a major-league restaurant in Seattle, New York or Los Angeles, for instance, could savor a meal of this salmon caught seventy-two hours earlier on the Copper River Flats. People who ate them, though, rarely knew more about the salmon than the name of the river. This time, I would carry the names of the fishermen, and their children and the town, too, with stories of the windy spring day she became food to all the people graced by her life.

The gale blew us into misery on the Copper River Flats that morning, but not before that beautiful king salmon arrived in our net. At that point, we were just the latest and most mortal in a chain of predators that testify to the immense resiliency of the creatures of the sea. I had to remind myself that while this particular fish was to be my food, millions of others compose the vibrant tapestry of life we call a salmon run, a collective being that is as naturally food as it is its own ancestor. So we bucked our way back to town, finally enjoying the lee of the mountain shore, the reliable pleasure of tying up to the dock at the fisherman's co-op

◄ *Pete Blackwell kisses his first salmon of the Bristol Bay season before throwing it back.*

▲ *Max McCarty proudly displays a Copper River salmon.*

Everybody oohed and aahed and a

couple of them reached out to pet the

salmon, savoring the slap of their hands

on the thick flesh under still-silver skin.

28

and the greeting for one special fish in the hold with the others.

We iced the salmon down in a big Styrofoam cooler, said our good-byes and I took her in a taxi to the airport. The cabby, who opened the cooler and pronounced the fish a "keeper," tore up the road on the fifteen-mile drive like he was carrying a freshly harvested organ to a transplant team. An hour later, we boarded a 737 jet like we were parading onto *Air Force One.* The captain, co-pilot, cabin crew and ground handlers met me at the door of the plane; we all shook hands and they invited me to ride on the flight deck. The salmon would be right behind us because the jet was a combination cargo and passenger liner with the freight section up forward. Before lashing the cooler to the floor, though, everybody took a look. This crew, which almost always hauled containers of salmon out of Cordova on this run, had plenty of reasons to be jaded about fish and fishing. Oddly, the moment turned into a kind of loopy nativity scene, right there in the cargo bay. Everybody oohed and aahed and a couple of them reached out to pet the salmon, savoring the slap of their hands on the thick flesh under still-silver skin. The co-pilot told his favorite salmon story, about the fifty-pounder he caught in Tacoma Narrows when he was a kid that almost pulled him out of the boat. One of the flight attendants bent over and sniffed at the fish. "It smells like a river," she said. "Musty, like earth, more than the ocean." I told them we'd caught her that morning on the Copper River Flats, and a few minutes later, we were airborne over the delta, punching in and out of the clouds, getting only the most momentary of glimpses below. We saw the boats, clusters of them in the tidal rivulets that fractured the enormous fan and sent flashes of sunlight ricocheting off the scud.

That night, in Seattle, the beautiful salmon seduced a restaurant chef, too, who prepared fillets in a half-dozen different combinations of herbs, butter, wine and garlic. He served us with the celebration usually reserved for embassy banquets, in honor of our distinguished guest. At one point, after he and his assistants finished serving and stood listening to us moan with delight while we ate, he stood almost at attention and said, "This fish would be honored to be food. It's a pleasure to know her."

At midnight, after lingering to hear every story anybody knew about salmon, we carried her remains out onto a dock in the warm spring night and returned them to the sea.

"This fish would

be honored to be food. It's a

pleasure to know her."

◄ *Salmon skeletons in a Canadian lake.*

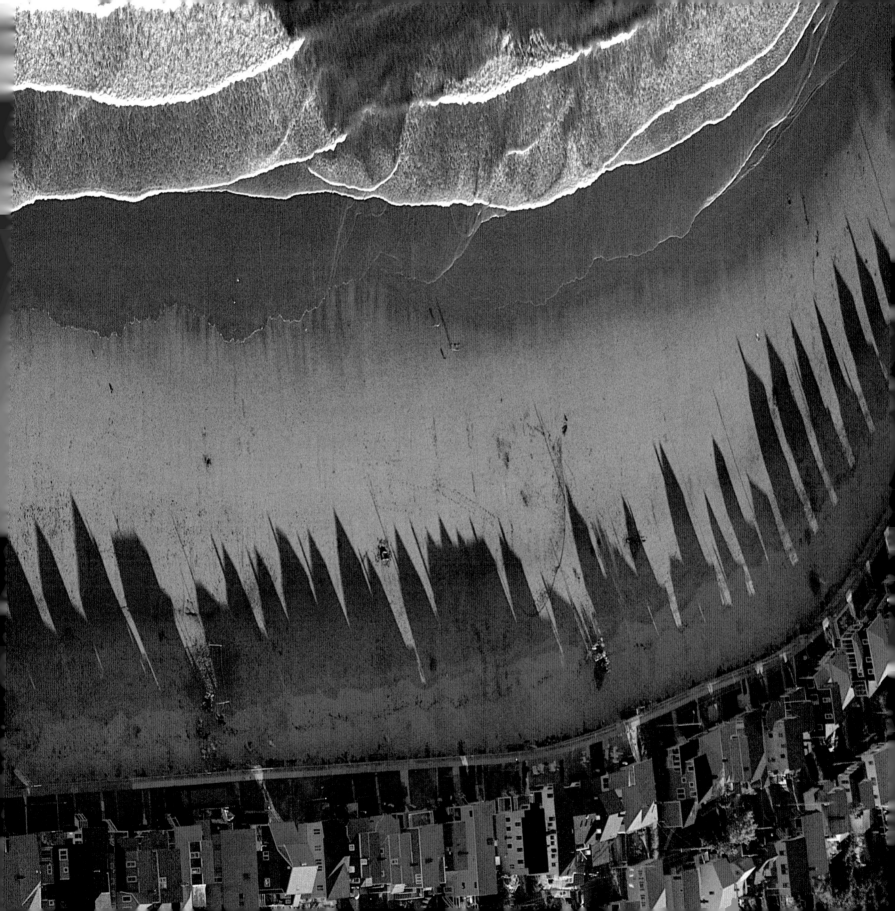

◄◄ *Half of the world's population lives within 60 miles of the coast, and the nearshore waters are*

loosing their ability to rebound from fishing pressure because of pollution and habitat destruction.

▲ *On guard at Marine Harvest's Noranjal farm in Ecuador.*

So What Have We Been Doing Wrong?

The wisdom of knowing where your food comes from was embedded in the routines of most early cultures and still in many modern cultures in which people still eat what they kill themselves. It was a lot easier to succumb to that kind of relationship when the earth was a resonant globe inhabited by a few million instead of a few billion. Despite our best intentions (it is probably wise to assume that no real evil is afoot), the bond between us and what feeds us dissolved in the steam and clatter of the industrial revolution and the subsequent radiation of humans beings into every habitable niche on the planet. Now, to sustain even what we're taking already from this newly finite ocean, we have to put the leash on three glaring abuses that would have been obvious more quickly in earlier times. It's not too late to adjust ourselves to the rhythms of food from the sea if we curb overfishing, waste less of what we do catch and guard the ocean habitat, particularly near shore, like our lives depended on it. Which, of course, they do.

Of those three abuses that deny us harmony with food from the sea, overfishing is the most obvious and potentially disastrous. I remember an afternoon meal in a Newfoundland outport with John and Mary Sullivan, their three sons, their wives, a swarm of children and platters of potatoes, mashed peas and pot roast. We talked about fishing, of course, since they were eight or ten generations into it there on the southern coast of an island that, for maybe a thousand years, has been synonymous with abundance from the sea. (Though the oceans occupy almost seven-eighths of the earth's surface, it is the continental shelves, invigorated by sunlight,

▲ *The collapse of the legendary cod stocks off Newfoundland devastated families that, for generations, had fished to live and lived to fish.*

Of those three abuses that

deny us harmony with food from the sea,

overfishing is the most obvious and

potentially disastrous.

33

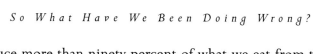

▲ *The Sullivan boys, off Newfoundland.*

Though people have overfished for

centuries, the scale of this [Atlantic cod]

disaster has never been matched.

that produce more than ninety percent of what we eat from the sea.) No place in history has more precisely defined the lively, churning coastal zone than the Grand Banks off Newfoundland, once the distant goal of fishermen from Europe, New England and the locals who chose or were compelled to winter over in that remote place. The North Atlantic over the banks is shallow, rarely more than six hundred feet deep, charged by the tidal engine and, until three decades ago, alive with fish. No longer.

The penalty for catching too many fish came to nonindustrial people like everything else about life, death, food and water: suddenly and obviously. To the fishing people of Newfoundland, the consequences of fishing too long, hard and irresponsibly were muted, the causes of collapsing stocks more vague. "We're all on the dole," John Sullivan told me. "They're paying us not to fish and we can't do a damn thing about it. It's not even our fault, Lord knows." Atlantic cod was once the mainstay of the Grand Banks and, to the south, George's Bank and the other once-productive fishing grounds. Now, commercial fishing for cod is completely banned off Newfoundland and nearly so off New England because there may not be enough left to recover from the steady decline. The breeding population is simply so small that it might never reach the ability to sustain itself at so-called commercial levels ever again. Though people have overfished for centuries, the scale of this disaster has never been matched.

But John Sullivan was only partly correct in saying that the collapse of the codfish is not the fault of fishermen like himself. For three decades after World War II, distant-water industrial fleets of trawlers and factory ships from hungry, recovering Europe and Asia hammered the offshore banks with virtually no limits. There was very little debate over the effects of such intensive fishing on the rest of the ecosystem and the seafloor. Very few people had ever heard the word "ecosystem" spoken at the time.

Then, in the mid-seventies, when Canada, the United States and every other nation with an ocean coast extended their political control two hundred miles from land, pressure from their own fleets allowed fishing to continue at far too great a pace. Armed with optimistic predictions of abundance and overseen only by managers from within the fishing community, local fishermen continued to catch what would prove to be too many codfish. Even when the collapse was apparent, the fishing communities of the North Atlantic insisted on their right to fish at historical levels.

But if you look at John Sullivan's denial another way, he could only know what everybody thought they knew when it came to codfish. Nobody really had a handle on how many he and the thousands of other fishermen could safely catch, and how many were on the banks. Part of the problem was, in fact, that most of the information on codfish came from people who had a stake in keeping the fleets on the grounds, not from people who perceived the food potential of the ocean as part of a larger, complex system. Finally, though, we are breaking free of this parochial approach to what we demand from nature. In just the past couple of decades, more of our fellow humans are deciding to step off the purely anthropocentric rock on which we have been standing for centuries. Instead, we are taking a look at ourselves as top predators woven into a complicated web with our food. This is a relationship not of dominance by humans, but one as full of the uncertainty, consequence and indifference to us as the rest of the cosmos.

Jane Lubchenco is a member of this new tribe of brave thinkers who no longer approach fisheries and the other of life's essentials we call natural resources only as they serve humankind. She is a marine biologist, teacher and, most consequential, an interdisciplinary thinker who lives most of the time in Oregon. "Fisheries have historically been approached with two

▲ *Cod jigging off Newfoundland.*

"First, the only thing people have cared about is what we can take out of a system; second, we believed the sea to be limitless."

▲ *Shrimping off Port Isabel, Texas.*

The problem: catching so many

fish that they can no longer sustain

populations large enough to

surrender food to us.

mind sets," she says. "First, the only thing people have cared about is what we can take out of a system; second, we believed the sea to be limitless. Another reason we reached a crisis point in fisheries is totally analogous with agriculture and forestry. The people who are giving advice about how much extraction the system can stand have very limited training in one specific area. And much of the advice that has been sought is of this sort: How do we catch more of X, and if X disappears, how do we switch over to catching Y and Z. Nobody was really thinking about the effects of removing X from the system. Hindsight is great, though, and it's easy to say we should have been thinking about fisheries in this way as opposed to that. We just didn't see the problems coming."

The problem: catching so many fish that they can no longer sustain populations large enough to surrender food to us. In 1997, according to scientists from the United Nations, all but two of the fifteen major oceanic fishing areas are now fished at or beyond their capacity, and four are actually in a state of decline. The Grand Banks and North Atlantic grounds are among the latter. On the Gulf of California off Mexico, the number of shrimp boats doubled from 1960 to 1980 and the catch dropped by 30%. Even in the United States, which has generally been able to manage fisheries more conservatively than many nations, 28% of the stocks within 200 miles of our coasts are overfished, 26% are being fished at the limit of capacity to produce sustainably, 12% could safely be fished more and the condition of the remaining 34% is unknown. The declines in some stocks are dramatic. In addition to the collapse of Atlantic cod, bluefin tuna have been fished so heavily that their spawning population is only 10 to 20% of what it was in 1970. Atlantic swordfish also have all but disappeared, and the ones that are caught are less than a third the size landed just twenty years ago.

Stopping the very real disaster that overfishing can bring is obvious: don't catch too many fish. That implies, though, that somehow we know how many are too many and, in some cases, we do. In other cases—swordfish for instance—we know very little about the animals we are eating, their breeding patterns, migration and the health of the food they eat, and we should make the most conservative decisions possible about catching any of them at all. Clearly, spending more of our global capital learning about what we catch instead of developing fishing power is one way to avoid overfishing.

A variety of national and international commissions and councils set catch quotas and manage the world's fishing fleets, and until just recently, almost no one outside the actual business of fishing played a part in those decisions. Now, though consumers, interdisciplinary scientists, environmental activists and other non-fishing people are making themselves heard. "Hey, wait a minute," they say. "You catch those fish, but we eat them so we're part of the system and we have a right to speak." Fisheries managers, therefore, are taking fewer risks when they set quotas and make the rules for fishing. Voter initiatives and lawsuits are becoming routine parts of the management scene as we all come to terms with the truths of a finite sea. And since what we catch has limits, the fishing fleets are finally being limited. This flies in the face of a deep cultural tradition in the fishing community that insists upon open access to the fishing grounds, an inalienable right to fish. Sadly, open access to many fishing grounds has already spelled disaster, but most industrial nations are quickly switching over to individual fishing quotas or limiting the number of licenses, type of gear and fishing time.

▲ *Gillnetting on the North Line, Bristol Bay, Alaska, an intensely competitive fishery that remains healthy because of limited access.*

. . . spending more of our global

capital learning about what we catch

instead of developing fishing power is

one way to avoid overfishing.

◄◄ *Shrimp fishermen off Cabo San Lucas, Mexico, where the shrimping gets worse every year.*

▲ *Aboard a shrimp boat near Port Isabel, Texas.*

Eat Everything on Your Plate

The dark partner of overfishing on oceans with a limited ability to sustain our demand for food is waste. Worldwide, we catch and throw away about 30 million tons of what could otherwise be edible food each year. That's a third of what we process and eat. In the fishing business, this waste is called "bycatch," and includes animals that are too young, too big, too small, too anything but what you want to take to market. Bycatch also includes catching animals like sea turtles, dolphins, whales, birds and any others that many people believe should not die or suffer injury to put seafood on our plates. Because dropping nets and hooks into the sea hoping to catch a meal is an uncertain proposition, bycatch will always exist. One of the keys to a harmonious relationship with seafood, though, is curbing what can only be called excess bycatch.

Take, for instance, the shrimp trawl fishery in most parts of the world. The routine aboard, say, a fifty-foot shrimper goes something like this: you set your nets, rigged from each side of the boat, and tow them along the bottom where the shrimp are. Then, with the help of hydraulic winches, you haul back, dump what you catch on deck and begin the backbreaking work of looking for shrimp. Bigger boats with sorters, and smaller shrimpers who simply poke through the shimmering mass of fish and, pick out the shrimp, shovel what's left back overboard. For every pound of shrimp that finds its way into a cocktail, pasta sauce or salad from a trawl, roughly ten pounds of fish and other potentially edible creatures die. That means that of the roughly 250 million pounds of shrimp caught by Gulf of Mexico and southern Atlantic trawlers, 2.5 billion pounds of something

▲ *For every pound of shrimp that makes it to a cocktail, four to ten pounds of fish and other sea life are thrown back into the sea, most of it dead.*

For every pound of shrimp that

finds its way into a cocktail, pasta sauce

or salad . . . roughly ten pounds of fish and

other potentially edible creatures die.

▲ *The king and queen rule over a shrimp festival in Biloxi, Mississippi.*

Pork producers say they use

everything but the squeal, and now fishing

fleets must move in the direction of using

everything but the splash.

else were thrown back into the sea, usually dead. Shrimp fisheries support thousands of nice people who are just trying to make a living, and if the sea were an infinite source of food, no problem. Bycatch that was acceptable twenty years ago when we were stumbling along with our admirable fiction of an infinite ocean is now completely out of the question. Pork producers say they use everything but the squeal, and now fishing fleets must move in the direction of using everything but the splash.

No shrimper or any other fisherman really wants to spend a lot of his time shoveling what he catches overboard, or killing turtles or dolphins that bring public relations nightmares down on him. In just the past fifteen years or so, pressure from consumers, government and environmental groups and innovative work by the fishing community has put the brakes on bycatch. Fishermen are as reluctant as the rest of us when it comes to changing habits and patterns, and some of the ways of curbing bycatch cost the fleets a lot of time and money. Most of the time, though, once the bycatch demon arrives, fishermen have directed their considerable energy and survival instinct toward solving the problem. The most celebrated bycatch success story came out of the distant-water tuna fleets that were killing thousands of dolphins every year in their nets. More canned tuna is sold than any other seafood, but unfortunately, in some areas of the world, schools of dolphins swim with the tuna. Whether you lived in Cleveland or Seattle, anybody with a child in elementary school in the 1980s remembers dolphin drawings and anti-fishing slogans. America's refrigerators were festooned with dolphin art which because of our cultural attachment to marine mammals became the object of a boycott of tuna fish. It worked. Consumers took responsibility for what they ate, put economic pressure on the fishing fleet, and in just a couple of years, the bycatch of dolphins by tuna seiners plummeted from several hundred thousand animals a year

to under 3,000. Under public pressure to change, the fleet figured out ways to free dolphins from the nets and, in most cases, avoid them altogether by setting their gear away from the mammals. They catch fewer tuna, but the kids aren't taping dolphin photos and slogans to their refrigerator doors any more.

The same kind of public outcry, backed by the Endangered Species Act, rose over the incidental killing of sea turtles by the shrimp fleet. Turtle excluder devices, called TEDs by the shrimpers who now must sew them into their nets, dramatically reduced the numbers of endangered turtles killed. A fisherman, Sinkey Boone from Georgia, was among those who led the way to the TED solution in the early 1970s when killing turtles to catch shrimp became obvious to him as a disaster waiting to happen. He and dozens of other shrimpers, state and federal fisheries agents and scientists figured out how to release turtles unharmed through a hatch in their nets, while keeping most of the shrimp inside. They had already been experimenting with excluder devices to cut down on the number of jellyfish

◄ *Spotted dolphins pace a shrimp boat in the eastern Pacific.* ▲ *A turtle excluder device (TED) rigged in a shrimp trawl.*

Turtle excluder devices, called TEDs

by the shrimpers who now must sew them

into their nets, dramatically reduced the

numbers of endangered turtles killed.

43

▲ *In 1969, Sinkey Boone designed a device to exclude turtles. Now he produces the "Georgia Jumper" TEDs like this one and teaches other shrimpers how to use them.*

"The thing you have to

understand . . . is that nobody wants to

catch fish that you can't sell or eat.

It's that simple."

and so-called "trash fish" to make each haul easier and more profitable. But not everybody figured out that shrimpers had a problem and TEDs were the solution. Because towing TEDs costs shrimpers money, a waterfront rebellion ignited when fisheries managers made TEDs mandatory on the Atlantic and Gulf coasts. But they worked, too, and the fleet kept fishing. By the mid-1990s, the United States banned imports of all shrimp taken in the waters of countries that do not require their shrimp trawlers to tow TEDs. This leveled the field for American shrimpers whose catch competes in the marketplace with shrimpers in other countries who, until then, had an advantage because they didn't use TEDs.

Shrimpers are also dealing with that unconscionable bycatch rate of fish and other creatures, which ranges from 400 to 1,000% or more per pound of landed shrimp. New technology, also developed in an inventive outburst by the shrimp fleet, dramatically reduces that rate by shunting fish through escape panels in the trawls. Several variations of the bycatch reduction devices—BRDs, for short, pronounced "birds"—have come out of garages and dock shacks from North Carolina to Texas, and now are mandatory on most shrimp grounds. "The thing you have to understand," said North Carolina shrimper, net builder and BRD inventor Bill Atkinson, "is that nobody wants to catch fish that you can't sell or eat. It's that simple. People really ought to stop thinking we want to harm the ocean for selfish reasons."

And in the large-scale industrial fisheries, managers are finally setting bycatch quotas that are increasingly more restrictive. North Pacific and Bering Sea groundfish trawlers and longliners working on Pacific cod, blackcod, yellowfin sole, rockfish and halibut usually hit their bycatch limits before their catch quota for the season. Soon, individual boats will likely have their own bycatch quotas, providing more incentive for each fisherman to "fish clean," as they say. Larger boats carry fisheries observers, who record the rate and amount of bycatch that comes aboard with each haul. When the fleet reaches its limit, fishing stops. Fishermen and their management councils, driven by pressure to cut bycatch, are turning to trawls with larger mesh sizes that let smaller fish go, and more hook-and-line fishing, which can be more selective. Bycatch reduction gear and methods are becoming as much a part of the fishermen's vernacular as nets, lines and bait.

Other kinds of "birds" are on fishermen's minds these days, too. Seabirds. Thorn Smith, a former abalone diver who now leads an association of freezer longliners that fish for cod and halibut, launched a campaign to avoid killing albatross on the North Pacific. "When I heard that members of my group had accidentally hooked and killed two short-tailed albatross in 1996, I knew we would eventually have a problem," Smith said. "That bird is not endangered because of fishing but because egg-pickers on their rookery islands near Japan almost killed them off thirty years ago, but fishermen will be blamed for the problem now. Only a few hundred breeding pairs remain, and we sincerely do not want to kill any of them."

Smith and others did research, got together with environmental groups and federal agencies and worked out a set of new rules requiring longliners to use devices to scare off the albatross and other seabirds. They handed the rules to the National Marine Fisheries Service and said, "Make us do this." Now, every longliner must rig at least one of several kinds of lines to scare away the birds, and also take other precautions when setting and retrieving their gear. They printed thousands of brochures that show longliners how to build bird-scaring gear, how to deploy it and why it mattered. "The truth is that we just don't want to be shut down because we're killing an endangered bird," Smith said. "It's not good for the birds, it's not good for business."

▲ *North Pacific longline fishermen devised gear and new rules to help reduce the mortality of albatross and other seabirds.*

"The truth is that we just don't want to be shut down because we're killing an endangered bird. . . . It's not good for the birds, it's not good for business."

45

◄◄ *Surf perch fishing off Central California.*

▲ *Coastal development costs more than purchasing a condominium.*

Living without Regret

▲ *You cannot build Los Angeles or Osaka and expect to have good fishing anywhere nearby.*

Because fishermen are really out there catching fish, shoveling bycatch, chasing away birds and dolphins and taking the risks of all seafarers on behalf of everyone who eats food from the sea, they alone cannot be held accountable for the crisis on the grounds. A big part of the challenge of achieving a long-term relationship with food from the sea is that fish and other marine life simply seem to be allergic to human beings and what we do to the sea, the coast and watershed. You cannot build Los Angeles or Miami, for instance, and expect to have good fishing anywhere in the vicinity. Fishermen may catch the last of the fish, but cities, dams, poorly managed agriculture and ruined coastal habitat are the big killers. Half of all the people in the world, roughly three billion of us, live within sixty miles of the coast, and the number is growing steadily. When there were fewer of us, the ocean was able to absorb, dilute and otherwise get rid of the debris and pollutants from a terrestrial population. Now, with so many of us huddled against the sea either living the good life or trying to survive, the ocean can't keep up with our waste.

As we urgently try to coax more food from the coastal zone, we may be introducing a new, destructive wrinkle to the food web. We humans have proven ourselves to be masters of domestication; in fact, seafood is the last major source of protein we get from wild animals. But one of the grave ironies about our attempt to boost the amount of food we get from the sea comes to us from fish farms. About 20% of our seafood today comes from farms, about 15 million tons all in all. The problem is that producing this food in large-scale marine sea farms is also destroying

Half of all the people in the world, roughly three billion of us, live within sixty miles of the coast, and the number is growing steadily.

▲ *"Things are fundamentally different on Earth than ever before in its history chiefly because of the enormous explosion of human population."* Jane Lubchenco

mangrove swamps and other vital elements of the coastal ecosystem. The shallows, estuaries and other life-support systems in the coastal zone nourish almost all the seafood we eat at some time during its development from egg to adult. In short, we are destroying the wildness we depend upon to produce food sustainably from the sea. Further complicating this dissonant impulse to domesticate seafood is the compound damage it does to the coasts in the nonindustrial world where most of the shrimp, salmon and shellfish farms are sprouting. People who depend on the sea to provide most of their protein are those who suffer most when sea farmers take over their nearshore habitat, depriving them of local seafood. To compound the problem, most of the food from large-scale sea farms is bought by consumers in the ten richest nations in the world, not by people who need it for basic survival. Our pride and power to domesticate seem to have hit the wall, though. The ocean is again telling us we can't expect it to be an infinite, resilient producer unless we defend marine habitat and build understanding based on the entire system rather than a single crop.

"More than anything else, we're going to have to change the way we think of the sea," Jane Lubchenco says. "Things are fundamentally different on Earth from ever before in its history chiefly because of the enormous explosion of human population. Fishing and the ocean must be viewed in a broader context of the changes that are happening in the world at large, and we have to look at the human population problem head-on. Nobody doubts that resources are finite anymore. We all know we are part of nature rather than in charge of it. Now, how do we learn from the past and do better in the future. The best thing we can do is to understand the system perspective, not just look at individual stocks, species and economic relationships."

▲ *Tiger prawns from one of Australia's well-managed, sustainable fisheries.*

"More than anything else,

we're going to have to change the

way we think of the sea."

▲ *Mangroves are critical habitat for the young of a host of commercially valuable fish.*

"The real choice is between

short-term prosperity and

long-term prosperity."

Finding ways to cross the rickety bridge between thousands of years of constant development and sustainability will not be easy. Though we are more aware of our excesses in the ocean environment, trying to curb overfishing, fishing with TEDs and BRDs, the problems associated with exploding human population and food from the sea are far from solved. The key to the future, according to Jane Lubchenco and others who keep their eyes wide open to the truth about our place in the food web, is taking a long-term perspective instead of the short term. "This garbage of jobs versus the environment, for instance, is a false dichotomy, the wrong way to look at the issue," says Lubchenco. "Historically, we believed that what we were getting from oceans is just tons of fish. Not only has this been the focus of management, but of public perception," she said. "Pretty much everybody—management and the public and fishermen themselves—have perceived things that way. And this is understandable. We are beginning to realize, though, that target species are connected to other species in the system. The response of the system to the removal of one species is often complex.

"The real choice is between short-term prosperity and long-term prosperity. Unfortunately, our economic systems are set up the wrong way. We have to change systems and natural resource accounting so we place a much higher premium not just on the market value of a particular fish but the full range of goods and services that comes from the ocean systems." The goods, as Lubchenco calls seafood, minerals and other sea products, are not the only things we get from the ocean. Focusing purely on those marketable commodities is a mistake. To have any chance at all of reaching a plateau of sustainability, we also have to value the services we get from the sea that are never taken directly to market. Climate control, for instance, is an enormous service provided to all life by the sea, and

 *Laborers in El Salvador plant mangrove seeds to restore a stretch of coastline.*

then there are the nourishing forces of the coastal shallows. The services that are provided to humans and all of life on earth are by-products of the functioning of the ecological system. When ecosystems are intact and healthy, a whole suite of services is the result."

Turning the tide on overfishing, bycatch and habitat destruction is a tall order. Most people don't determine fishing quotas, make resource policy or limit the amount of international corporate investment that drives overfishing and abusive sea farming; however, they are genuinely concerned about the state of the environment. We know from issues such as recycling and dolphin-safe tuna that people are willing to help if it will do some good. We know, now, we have to be responsible for everything about the food we eat, where it came from, who caught it for us and how many are left to produce new generations for our children and their children. That delicate fillet of Pacific cod, luscious piece of dill and garlic salmon or shrimp salad you eat tonight is, really, the whole ocean.

That delicate filet of Pacific cod,

luscious piece of dill and garlic salmon

or shrimp salad you eat tonight is,

really, the whole ocean.

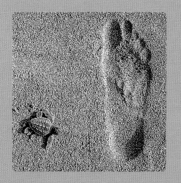

"One of the great

dreams of man must

be to find some place

between the extremes of

civilization and nature

where it is possible to

live without regret."

—Barry Lopez

THE GLOBAL DILEMMA

For thousands of years, until the Twentieth Century, people who fished were on much more even footing with the food they took from the ocean. They cast nets woven painstakingly from natural fibers, set hooks fashioned from bone or brittle steel and employed only muscle power or the simplest of levers to retrieve their gear and the fish. They ventured offshore only as far as sails, oars and paddles could take them, and were at great risk every time they went to sea. The arrival of engines, synthetic line, nets and other modern fishing tools in virtually every fishery in the world signaled the end of that parity. Human beings have gained an enormous advantage and we seem to have disturbed the balance in the natural dance of predator and prey. Through all of human history until 1946, we never took more than 20 million metric tons from the sea in any year; from 1950 to 1989, our catch increased to 90 million metric tons.

◄ *Net mending, Morocco.*

▲ *A Bedodouzan weaves grass into rope*
to make a fishing net, Morocco.

57

▲ *Industrial-scale fishing off their coasts means local fishermen in Senegal and around the world face declining catches.*

◄ On the beach in Senegal, locals compete with commercial buyers for fish.

▲ Artisanal fisheries often are self-limiting simply because of the danger of going to sea.

▲ *A pirogue, Senegal.*

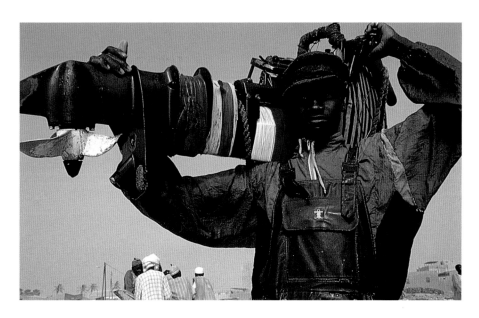

◄ *A Senegalese fisherman with his most prized asset—an outboard motor.*

▲ *Fish market, Senegal.*

▲▲ *Moray eels on display, Morocco.*

▲ *Freshly caught fish, Madagascar.*

▶ *Senegalese fishermen meet buyers from Dakar on the beach.*

▲ *A large yellowfin tuna is hauled over the rail off Cape Verde Island.*

▲ *Victoria Market, Mahé, Seychelles.*

▲▲ *Surf fishermen, Santiago, Praia.*

▲ *Chokomey market, Ghana.*

CATCHES ARE FALLING

Since 1973, catches in the Atlantic and Pacific oceans, Mediterranean and Black seas actually have been in steady decline. Only in the Indian Ocean, where fisheries are limited by more primitive technologies and methods, are landings on the rise, increasing by about five percent per year. Worldwide, about 200 million people depend directly on fishing for their livelihoods, and in many cases, survival. Fisheries collapse, whether from fishing pressure or natural cycles of abundance, and can mean famine and malnutrition in regions where people depend heavily upon locally available protein from the sea. In the highly industrialized world, when fish is not available, we just buy chicken, pork or beef.

◄ AND ▲ *The local fleet, Vizhinjam, India.*

▲ *Near Vizhinjam, India.*

▶ *Poor fishing off Vizhinjam, India.*

▲ *Fishermen display their catch off the coast of Vizhinjam, India.*

A WORLD ON A DIET

Food from the sea contributes only one percent to the global economy in terms of cash, but it adds more protein to the world supply than any other animal source. The ratio of seafood to total protein need varies widely from region to region. As recently as 1988, seafood made up about 28% of the diet of a person living in Asia and Indonesia. In Africa, 21% percent of a person's protein comes from the sea; in Western Europe, about 10%; in Latin America, about 8%; in North America, about 7%. The average consumption of protein produced by the sea around the world is about 16%. What this means, though, is that people in the non-industrial world who eat more aquatic protein per pound of food are placed at enormous risk if we over-fish, waste seafood and degrade ocean habitat.

▲ *A Vietnamese woman sells breakfast to returning fishermen in the harbor of Phan Thiet, Vietnam.*

▶ *The fishing fleet, Mui Ne Harbor, Vietnam.*

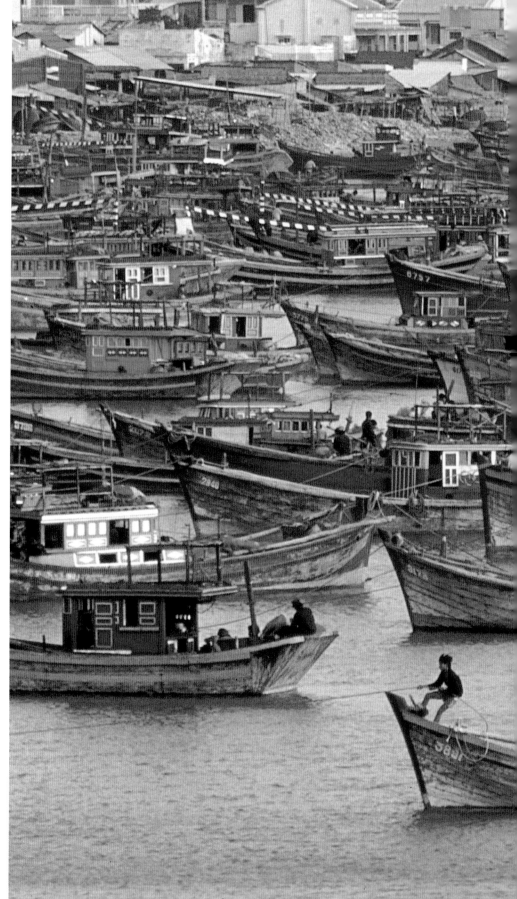

▲ *Hat Yai, Thailand.*

▶ *Drying fish, Hat Yai,*

Thailand.

▲ AND ▶ *On a village dock in Thailand, fishermen*

prepare shrimp paste.

▲ *Floating market, Thailand.*

▲ *Floating market, Thailand.*

▲ *Chinese fishermen train cormorants to dive for fish, putting rings around the birds' necks to keep them from eating their catch.*

▲ *Seahorses for sale, Cebu, Philippines.*

▲ *Reef diving off the coast of Roxas in the Philippines.*

▲ *A dump called Smokey Mountain in Manila Bay, Philippines,*

unfortunately, a typical abuse of the coastal zone.

▲ *Unloading at Brundong, Java, Indonesia.*

▲ *Indonesian women dig clams to feed their families and to sell at the local market.*

▲ *Preparing clams, Borneo.*

▲ *At Cheung Chau Island, Hong Kong, the day's catch hangs drying in the sun.*

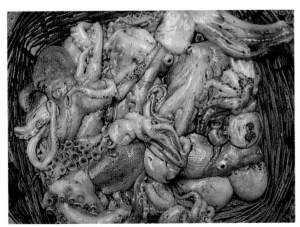

▲▲ AND ▲ *A basket of octopus, Cheung Chau Island.*

▲▲ *A fish market, Hong Kong.*

▲ *Fish market, Mong Kok, Hong Kong.*

◄ AND ▲ *Fresh fish for sale in night markets in Mong Kok, Hong Kong.*

▲ *Japanese fish brokers carefully inspect salmon at a plant in Iwate Prefecture.*

▲ *Opening a ceremony in Sapporo, Japan, Sute Orita carries the season's first salmon.*

▲ *Tuna being prepared to sell in a Japanese fish market.*

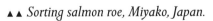
▲▲ *Sorting salmon roe, Miyako, Japan.*

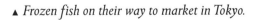
▲ *Frozen fish on their way to market in Tokyo.*

▲ *Tuna, Tsukiji Market, Tokyo.*

▲ *Fishing boats in the harbor, Vigo, Spain.*
▲▶ *At fishing docks in Spain, shark (top right) and swordfish (bottom) are among the many varieties of seafood that await processing and shipment around the world.*

▲ *Shark and swordfish, Vigo, Spain.*

▲ *Along Ria de Bilbao, Spain, a man digs for worms in front of the Altos Hornos de Vizcaya Company.*

▲ *Crabs ready to go to market.*

▲ *Fishermen in Limones harvesting shrimp in their handmade nets.*

CHANGING THE RULES

The boundaries and rules for fishing on the world's oceans have changed in the past two decades as dramatically as the post-Cold War geopolitical map. Almost every nation has extended its sovereignty out to 200 miles from the coast, and we are enjoying a bloom of unprecedented international collaboration. The United Nations has proposed a covenant for responsible fishing that will likely be signed by the governments of most fishing countries, and major treaties governing fisheries in international waters are in place. Though disputes are as common as resolution in global fisheries politics, fishing nations finally realize that unilateral development in their own waters and off the shores of nonindustrial countries will soon be history.

▲ *Salmon fisherman, Magadan, Russia.*

▶ *Salmon fishing, Sakhalin Island, Russia.*

▲ *A classic example of the modern factory trawler, capable of catching and processing hundreds of tons of cod, pollock and other fish, Bering Sea, Alaska.*

▶ *On the Bering Sea pollock grounds, near the Islands of Four Mountains.*

▲ *A full codend of Bering Sea pollock, maybe 150 tons on deck.*

◄ *Not much survives the trip to the surface in a trawl, and the heavy industrial fleets around the world kill billions of pounds of fish each year that never make it to the table.*

▲ *A factory trawler off Iceland.*

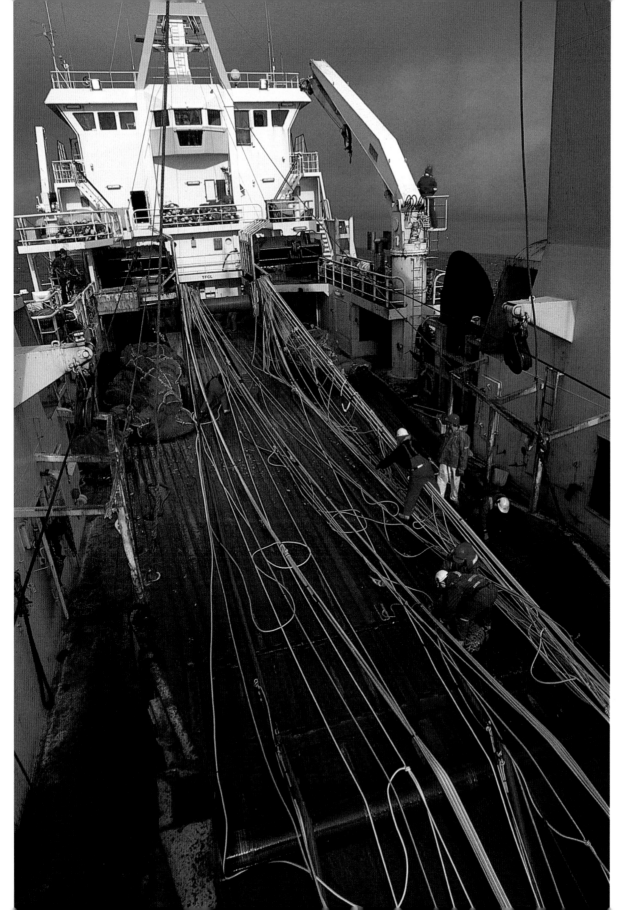

◄ Hauling back a large
midwater trawl.
▲ Aboard the factory
trawler Svalbakur,
off Iceland.

▲ Narragansett Bay, Rhode Island.

► Fishermen releasing a leatherback turtle,
Narragansett Bay, Rhode Island.

▲ *An ocean sunfish taken as bycatch off Rhode Island.*

DOING THE RIGHT THING

Though this may come as a surprise to many, North American fisheries scientists and fishermen are leading the world in adjusting to the realities of a finite amount of protein from the sea. Alaskan salmon fisheries have a big advantage over those in other regions because they are not pressured by the habitat destruction typical in Korea, Japan and the North American West Coast. But there, too, the people voted to limit the number of boats in their fleets, and the salmon runs have been setting records every year. Other American and Canadian fisheries are following suit, and in Europe, too, the idea of limiting access to the grounds is taking hold. The United States has also made inroads into curbing the bycatch of endangered species, including dolphins and sea turtles, by insisting that trading nations abide by the rules to protect these animals, or suffer sanctions.

◄ *The gillnet fleet, Bristol Bay, Alaska.*

▲ *Hauling back, Bristol Bay, Alaska.*

▲ *Fishing for a living is twenty-four times more dangerous than coal mining.*

▲ *Salmon trolling, Southeast Alaska.*

▶ *Halibut longlining, Gulf of Alaska.*

▲▲ *Picking a gillnet, Bristol Bay, Alaska.*

▲ *Salmon roe, a delicacy, is salted and shipped to Japan.*

▶ *Aboard a salmon tender, Bristol Bay, Alaska.*

▲ AND ▶ *Beach cleanup crew, after the* Exxon Valdez *disaster, Prince William Sound, Alaska.*

DOWN ON THE FARM

Farming fish, shrimp and shellfish in the sea can add millions of tons of protein to the global diet, but only if it is done responsibly. The ocean and coastal systems are best viewed as storehouses of kinetic food energy, and we have to conserve and protect the mangroves, intertidal zones and estuaries from destructive farming in addition to fishing responsibly. In Ecuador, a shrimp farming boom began in the early 1960s and between 1975 and 1985, the South American nation has led the world, producing national income of more than $225 million and creating 150,000 jobs. Unfortunately, building the shrimp farms destroyed thousands of acres of mangroves that are crucial to a healthy coastal zone and rearing area for dozens of other species. Smaller farms that raise several species and don't destroy other parts of the ecosystem are ways to end abusive farming.

▲ *Where mangrove forests used to grow, armed guards now patrol Ecuadorian shrimp ponds, guarding against attack by local villagers.*

▶ *Fishermen north of Esmeraldas, Ecuador.*

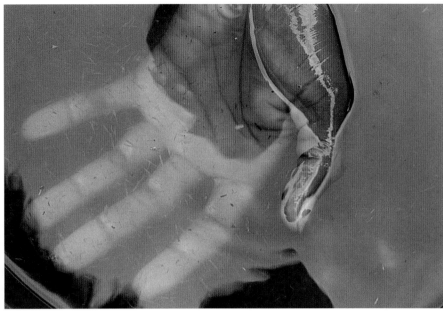

◄ *Night fishing for gravid shrimp, near Tonchique, Ecuador.*

▲ *Wild shrimp larvae, Ecuador.*

▲ *In Tonchique, Ecuador, lavaderos use butterfly nets to catch shrimp larvae.*

◂ *Along the Mosquito Coast, Nicaragua, green sea turtles are caught and taken to market.*

▲ *Sanctions now await fishermen from all nations who sell shrimp to the United States, unless they use turtle excluder devices (TEDs) in their trawls.*

◄ AND ▲ *Turtle hatchlings,*
ready for the sea.

117

American Fisheries Society, World Aquaculture Society and National Shellfisheries Association. *Aquaculture '95 Book of Abstracts.* Washington, D.C.: American Fisheries Society, 1995.

Alverson, Dayton L., Mark H. Freeberg, Steven A. Murawaski and J.P. Pope. A Global *Assessment of Fisheries Bycatch and Discards.* Rome: FAO, 1994.

Bardach, John E., John H. Ryther and William O. McLarney. *Aquaculture: The Farming and Husbandry of Freshwater and Marine Organisms.* NY: Wiley-Interscience, A Division of John Wiley & Sons, Inc., 1972.

Benetti, Daniel D., Arietta Venizelos and Carlos Acosta. "Finfish Aquaculture Development in Ecuador." *World Aquaculture,* 25(2), 1994.

Brown, Lester R. and Hal Kane. *Full House: Reassessing the Earth's Population Carrying Capacity.* NY: W.W. Norton & Company, 1994.

Center for Marine Conservation.

Fish for the Future: A Citizen's Guide to Federal Marine Fisheries Management. Washington, D.C.: Center for Marine Conservation, 1993.

_____. *Delay and Denial: A Political History of Sea Turtles and Shrimp Fishing.* Washington, D.C.: Center for Marine Conservation, 1995.

Committee on Biological Diversity in Marine Systems. *Understanding Marine Biodiversity: A Research Agenda for the Nation.* Washington, D.C.: National Academy Press, 1995.

Earle, Sylvia A. *Sea Change: A Message of the Oceans.* NY: G.P. Putnam's Sons, 1995.

Food and Agriculture Organization, Fishery Resources and Environment Division. *Review of the State of World Fishery Resources.* Rome: Food and Agriculture Organization of the United Nations, 1992.

Leet, William S., Christopher M. Dewees and Charles W. Haugen, eds. *California's Living Marine Resources*

and Their Utilization. CA: California Sea Grant Extension, 1992.

Meadows, Donella H., Dennis L. Meadows and Jørgen Randers. *Beyond the Limits: Confronting Global Collapse, Envisioning a Sustainable Future.* VT: Chelsea Green Publishing Company, 1992.

Norse, Elliott A., ed. *Global Marine Biological Diversity: A Strategy for Building Conservation into Decision Making.* Washington, D.C.: Island Press, 1993.

Rosenberry, Bob, ed. *Aquaculture Digest.* CA: Bob Rosenberry, 1993.

Rosenthal, Harald. "Aquaculture and the Environment." *World Aquaculture,* 25(2), 1994.

Safina, Carl. *Scientific American.* 1995.

Upton, Harold F., Peter Hoar and Melissa Upton. *The Gulf of Mexico Shrimp Fishery: Profile of a Valuable National Resource.* Washington, D.C.: Center for Marine Conservation, 1992.

U.S. Department of Commerce, National Oceanic and Atmospheric Administration and National Marine Fisheries Service. *Fisheries of the United States, 1993.* MD: U.S. Department of Commerce, 1994.

Weber, Michael L. and Judith A. Gradwohl. *The Wealth of Oceans.* NY: W.W. Norton & Company, 1995.

Weber, Peter. *Abandoned Seas: Reversing the Decline of the Oceans.* Washington, D.C.: Worldwatch Institute, 1993.

_____. *Net Loss: Fish, Jobs, and the Marine Environment.* Washington, D.C.: Worldwatch Institute, 1994.

Wieland, Robert. *Why People Catch Too Many Fish: A Discussion of Fishing and Economic Incentives.* Washington, D.C.: Center for Marine Conservation, 1992.

World Resources Institute (WRI). *A Guide to the Global Environment.* NY: Oxford University Press, 1994.

Worldwatch Institute. *State of the World 1995.* NY: W.W. Norton & Company, 1995.

M O N T E R E Y   B A Y   A Q U A R I U M   P R E S S

886 Cannery Row   Monterey, CA 93940   www.mbayaq.org

QTY. TITLE	SKU	UNIT PRICE	QTY. TITLE	SKU	UNIT PRICE			TOTAL COST
SANCTUARY BOOKS			___*Sea Searcher's Handbook: Activities from the Monterey Bay Aquarium*	47138	$16.95	*For shipping and postage charges for US address only, ADD the following amounts:*		
___*A Natural History of the Monterey Bay National Marine Sanctuary*	86510	$19.95	___*Young Explorer's Guide To Undersea Life*	92508	$16.95			
NATURAL HISTORY BOOK SERIES						$0-15.00 add $3.95		
___*Elkhorn Slough*	13716	$ 9.95	**EXHIBIT-RELATED BOOKS**			$15.01 - 30.00 add $5.95		
___*Gray Whales*	16515	$ 9.95	___*A Guide to the World of the Jellyfish*	17212	$ 5.95	$30.01 - 50.00 add $6.95		Subtotal _____
___*Kelp Forests*	13717	$ 9.95	___*Monterey Bay Aquarium (souvenir book)*	18503	$ 6.95	$50.01 - 75.00 add $8.95		Shipping_____
___*Octopus and Squid*	47155	$ 9.95	___*The Outer Bay*	92491	$ 4.95	$75.01 - 100.00 add $9.95		
___*Sea Otters*	14746	$ 9.95				$100.00+ add $12.95		Sales Tax_____
___*Seals and Sea Lions*	23624	$ 9.95	**VIDEOS**			*Rush delivery? Alaska, Hawaii, or International destinations? Please call for shipping charges*		
___*Seashore Life on Rocky Coasts*	18813	$ 9.95	___*Behind-the-Scenes at the Monterey Bay Aquarium*	47172	$24.95			TOTAL _____
___*Sharks and Rays*	14745	$ 9.95	___*Jellies and Other Ocean Drifters*	22964	$19.95	HOW TO ORDER		
FOR KIDS			___*The Monterey Bay Aquarium Video Treasury*	12815	$24.95	Contacting our Gift and Bookstore.		
___*Flippers & Flukes Marine Mammals Coloring Book*	47121	$ 3.95				MONTEREY BAY AQUARIUM GIFT AND BOOKSTORE		
___*Sea Life Coloring Book*	47104	$ 3.95				TEL (408) 648-4952 FAX (408) 648-4994 EMAIL giftstore@mbayaq.org E-QUARIUM www.mbayaq.org		

It's important to realize that,

while fisheries around the world are in trouble,

it's not too late to turn the tide.

—Julie Packard